The Seven R's of Great Gr

Also in this series

Also by Sue Cowley

The Seven R's of Great Group Work

SUE COWLEY

Sue Cowley Books Ltd

2013

Sue Cowley Books Ltd
PO Box 1172
Bristol BS39 4ZJ

www.suecowley.co.uk

© **Sue Cowley Books Ltd**

First published 2013

Part of the 'Alphabet Sevens' Series

Also in this series:

The Seven C's of Positive Behaviour Management
The Seven T's of Practical Differentiation
The Seven P's of Brilliant Voice Usage

ISBN: 978-1493523108

Contents

Introduction

Group work has the potential to be a brilliant strategy for learning, with many benefits for students. However, it is a tricky technique to use well, and there are a number of potential pitfalls. For group work to be 'great', the teacher has to manage, structure and focus the activity so that the best possible learning can take place. We cannot simply put our students into groups and leave them to work without guidance or support. If we do, we run the risk that, while the children are working within a group format, they are not working *as* a collaborative group.

This mini guide will help you get the very best out of group work, whatever age group or subject area you teach. In this book you will find practical ideas and techniques to make your group work as 'great' as it can possibly be. As with all my books, this guide is full of strategies that you can put to use straight away. You will also find specific examples throughout this book of great group work activities.

Group work helps your students develop many different skills and attitudes, ones that are highly valued in the world beyond school. They build their collaborative skills, develop language, explore ideas and learn how to share and take turns. When working in groups, students develop their social skills, 'rehearse' their thinking out loud and hear it critiqued, learn how to negotiate roles and how to act as leaders. They also understand when it might work best to delegate tasks or responsibilities. Group work builds a feeling of community: the students are the crew building learning with the teacher, rather than the passengers on a teacher driven train.

Research has shown that group work is an effective way for students to build their cognitive skills*. Group work boosts relationships between the teacher and his or her students, and helps children actively engage in what they are learning. There are some curriculum areas in which group work is an integral part of the subject itself. In these subjects the ability to work with and alongside others is vital for success. These 'group work based' subjects include drama, dance and key areas within physical education.

In many ways, it is simpler for the teacher or the students to work alone. When we learn individually, we can focus on our own needs and desires. We can be passive recipients of learning or even switch off from learning altogether. But human beings are naturally sociable – we love to chat and share ideas and build on each other's thinking. For many teachers, group work instinctively feels like a great method to use with their classes.

Group work is a complex teaching structure. It is a tricky strategy for an educator to manage effectively, and it is also hard for students to do well. Some teachers may lack confidence in using group work, and perhaps shy away from it as a result. But just because group work is difficult to do well, this is no reason not to use it. This concise guide will help you maximise the learning that takes place when you use group work with your students.

Sue Cowley
www.suecowley.co.uk

* www.tlrp.org/pub/documents/no11_blatchford.pdf

The First R:

Reasons

The First R: Reasons

When you ask your students to work in a group, there should be a valid reason for the activity to happen in this format. Your reason for using a group might be to do with the area of the subject or topic you are teaching; it might be linked to key skills or attributes that you want your students to develop. You and your students should be clear about why the activity is happening in a group, and also about what kind of outcomes you can hope to achieve as a result of doing the group task.

Some subjects lend themselves perfectly to group work. In a subject such as drama, group work is the main format in which the students learn, because (monologues aside) drama is about the ability to perform collaboratively. Group work is vital within team sports as well: a key aspect of a successful sports team is the ability to play well together.

In early years settings and primary schools, a group or class of children learn together for a whole academic year, and sometimes longer. There is usually one regular class teacher, or group of practitioners and it is therefore vital for the adults to build strong relationships with their children. It is also critical that the children learn to work cooperatively with others in the class, for the success of the group as a whole over the course of the year.

This 'one group' effect is less pronounced at secondary level, because the class make-up may vary from subject to subject. The students have a number of different teachers, rather than a single one. Each teacher has more children to teach, and therefore less time and opportunity to form a close bond with any single class. In many ways the role of the form tutor replicates the primary class/teacher relationship – the tutor focuses on the social and emotional aspects of learning, which in turn support each child's academic achievement.

Although some subjects clearly lend themselves to group work more than others, it is important to develop collaborative learning in all subjects of the curriculum. In the same way that we now understand the importance of boosting literacy in subjects other than English, so we can boost our students' collaborative skills by introducing group work into all subjects.

Reasons for Group Work

There are many different, and valid, reasons why you might ask your students to do an activity in a group format. Often, there will be several benefits in using a collaborative approach. Group work involves people sharing and building on each other's ideas, and therefore it is most likely to be beneficial in tasks that are aimed at building conceptual understanding together. A group format is particularly useful for activities that rely on the use of skills like problem solving, reasoning, interpretation and inference.

Your reasons to use group work might include that:

✓ It is the best way to teach a specific area of the curriculum, for instance learning how to consider different viewpoints in PSHE or devising an improvised piece in drama;
✓ You need or want to boost skills such as cooperation, consideration, empathy and turn taking;
✓ The learning demands it – for instance where 'creative collaboration' is a key part of the learning objective;
✓ You want to boost the children's speaking and listening skills (which will feed into their success in all different subject areas);

- ✓ You would like more children to have their voices heard, and to practise articulating their ideas, but there is only one of you and perhaps thirty or more of them;
- ✓ You want to utilise a sense of competition and consequently enhance motivation – group can compete against group without the pressure of individual competition;
- ✓ There is an issue with limited resources, and by putting the students in groups you can give them all a chance to use different resources;
- ✓ It is an effective strategy for differentiation, for instance where children work together in groups with a similar reading age, you can vary the complexity of the texts used by each group;
- ✓ The students desperately need to build their cooperative skills, especially if uncooperative attitudes are spilling over into other aspects of their time with you;
- ✓ The children need to build their social and language skills, and incorporating some group work will help them to achieve this;
- ✓ It takes the pressure off you a bit, and refocuses the students on taking responsibility for their own learning;
- ✓ The children need variety in the formats in which they learn, and so do you: group work provides a welcome change to a diet of whole class teaching and individual learning.

'Real Life' Reasons

As well as the teacher having valid reasons to use group work, you can also create group work that has (or pretends to have) a valid reason in real life. This might mean having a real audience for the learning that the students are doing, or it could be that you incorporate aspects of life beyond the school gates into the activities that they do.

When a group task feels connected to a topical or a real life situation, the students are likely to focus and engage with it. For those students who have become cynical or disaffected about what school can offer them, connecting learning to the reality of life beyond the school gates is a useful motivator. The question 'what use is this to me when I leave school?' is one that disaffected students ask. If you can point out a direct link to real life, this provides an answer to that question.

There are many ways in which you can bring a sense of reality into group tasks. For instance, you might use:

✓ Newspaper clippings about a topical news story to show your students how their studies link to real world events;
✓ Case studies to show how 'real people' are impacted by our decisions;
✓ A topic that is of real interest to the students outside of school, as a basis for the activities;
✓ 'Real life' audiences for the students' work – for instance, working in groups to create a magazine for a younger year group in the school;
✓ Visitors from the real world who work in teams/groups (police, paramedics, sportsmen and women, etc.);
✓ Trips to the world beyond the classroom to utilise collaboration, for instance getting your students to work as a team on a local environmental project.

For Example: Show your students how group work can have real world impact by using this charity group activity, perhaps as a primary class or tutor group challenge, or as a project across the whole school. Explain to the students that each group is going to be given £10 with which to raise money for a charity, within a set time frame. The students can spend their money in whatever way they decide is best, and the 'winning' group is the one that raises the most money for the charity.

Role of the Expert

When using the 'role of the expert' technique, the teacher asks the students to work as experts to solve a problem, to come to conclusions or to approach a specific scenario. Often, 'role of the expert' scenarios involve the students in lateral thinking and in making decisions. Again, this gives a sense of reality and a real life purpose to group work. The drama teacher Dorothy Heathcote called this technique the 'mantle of the expert'.

The 'expert' role might be:

✓ As professionals within a particular field (a team of doctors, a group of police detectives, a team of personnel managers, a group of travel agents);
✓ As characters from fiction, or from the past (a group of historical figures from a particular time period, or a set of characters from a book or a story);
✓ A group of people within a specific scenario, all with differing talents (some travellers whose plane has crash landed on a desert island, a management team running a new pop group).

For Example: The Personnel Managers' Dilemma

In this scenario the students work as personnel managers, in response to a difficult dilemma. I have used it for speaking and listening work in English; it would also work well for a business studies course. The students are given the details of a range of employees who work for a company. The information includes salary, benefits (e.g. company car), personal background, length of service, and so on.

The teacher explains to the team of personnel managers that they have been brought in to save the company a specific amount of money. They must decide how to go about this: will they make some employees redundant, will they cut benefits or will they lower salaries? The activity can encourage lateral thinking, and it can also be used to explore employment law, for instance the legalities around making staff redundant or changing pay and conditions.

Project Based Learning

Where the students are given an element of choice about what they would like to work on within their groups, this can enhance their levels of motivation. During a project, the students are asked to take responsibility for their own learning, and for the success of the group as a whole. They can extend the learning as far as they wish: there are no limits to how broad, rich and deep their responses will be. You might leave the contents of the project fairly open-ended, or you could give your groups a series of tasks to complete.

The students could focus their project on:

✓ A specific area within a wider aspect of a subject or topic. For instance you could ask groups to choose one aspect of settlements within Geography to look at in detail, or to focus on a country within the continent you are studying.

✓ An 'expert group' scenario, for instance working as 'Pop Group Managers' to manage a music group. This could include writing songs, designing CD covers, writing articles for a pop magazine, and so on.

✓ Developing a product for a specific purpose, for example as part of a business studies topic, as a design and technology challenge or as an artistic creation for a display.

The Second R:

Roles

The Second R: Roles

When you use group work there is always the danger that some children will take over the running of the group, while others hitch a ride on the backs of their more confident or well-motivated peers. The teacher can manage and mitigate this issue through skilful organisation and careful interventions. In addition, the teacher can help the children learn to take on new roles that challenge them, to extend their thinking or to build their social and emotional skills.

One very useful way to structure and focus group activity is to ensure that the students take on appropriate roles. These roles should offer the right level of challenge to students, helping them stay focused on the learning activity that has been set. The way that we decide what is 'appropriate' might depend on an objective we want them to achieve (for instance 'to gain confidence') or on the learning that we want to happen. You can decide on the roles that the students will take within a group; you can encourage the students to decide on what roles they wish to take on individually; or you can ask them to choose within their groups.

If your students are used to working in a competitive environment, where it is usually 'everyone for themselves', they may find it hard at first to participate as an equal member of a group. Set clear expectations of how you want them to behave before any group work begins. Gradually they will learn to take a more cooperative approach to learning.

Strategies for Allocating Roles

There are many ways to decide on or to indicate the different roles that you want the students to take within their groups. The method you choose will vary according to the task you are setting, the outcomes you want to achieve, and also on your knowledge of the individuals within the class. When defining roles, you could:

✓ Allocate specific roles yourself, based on your knowledge of your students and what you want them to achieve within the group work;

✓ Ask the students to allocate the roles within their group, based on the idea of setting themselves a challenge – you might ask them to 'choose a role that you know you find hard or an area that you want to develop';

✓ Use a random method to allocate roles;

✓ Ask the students to undertake different roles for a set period of time, moving around so that they experience a variety of perspectives.

To add a bit of creativity to the allocation of roles, you can use:

✓ Playing cards, with different suits or different numbered cards indicating different roles. For instance, the person who picks the Ace could be the group leader.

✓ Cards with different kinds of animals to indicate the role that the child should take on. This is fun with younger children as it offers them a symbolic representation of what the role involves. For instance, the 'owl' could be the wise person who brings expert knowledge to the table, while the 'squirrel' could hunt around for resources.

✓ Job descriptions of different roles, where you give a brief outline of the activities that should be done by someone who takes on this role. To add some fun, you could create 'Top Trumps' style cards showing the attributes of each role.

If your group task or project is going to take several lessons to complete, consider asking students to move roles within their group, during the course of the activity.

Simple Roles

The kind of roles you ask students to take on will depend on their age, and also on their experience of working within groups. At first your students may struggle to work within larger groups, or to undertake complex roles. Begin by asking them to take on simple roles or to work within very small group units (pairs or threes). In these small units, it is much easier for quiet students to contribute. As the students gain confidence in working together you can gradually increase the size of groups and the complexity of group tasks.

Talk Partners

This is a very simple group activity, useful for short discussions, particularly during whole class time. The teacher asks a question and the children turn to a partner to discuss their ideas. Once they have had a couple of minutes to do this, the teacher picks a student to share what their pair discussed, or the children feed back as a whole class.

Think – Pair – Share

This is similar to talk partners, but the students take a short time to think about their own ideas, before they share them with a partner, and then with the whole class.

Idea Tennis

This works well for when you want the students to come up lots of ideas. Put the children into pairs and then ask them to bounce their ideas backwards and forwards like a game of tennis. The first person gives an idea, then the second person gives another idea in response, and so on.

Triads

A triad is a group of three students working together. This simple set up offers a clearly defined set of roles for the students to use. For discussion tasks, one person takes on the role of the speaker, another person works as the questioner, and the other acts as the recorder. The students can swap over their roles during the course of the activity, or as defined by the teacher.

During a discussion triad:

✓ The Speaker makes a statement about an issue or gives an explanation;
✓ The Questioner ensures clarity or encourages depth by asking questions of the speaker;
✓ The Recorder makes notes about what is said, and reports back to the group or the class at the end of the group work session.

You can adapt the Triad group structure for different subject areas. For instance, in PE your triad might be made up of:

✓ A Player who demonstrates a skill or movement within the particular area of sport;
✓ A Coach who gives advice to help the Player develop;

✓ An Umpire who ensures that the correct rules are followed.

2 – 4 – 8

This technique is sometimes referred to as 'snowballing'. It offers a gradual build-up in the size of the groups. This ensures that all children have the chance to contribute in smaller groups at first, and that ideas can be shared around amongst the students.

✓ Start by setting a question or research task and asking the students to discuss it in pairs;
✓ After a while, get each pair to join up with another pair, to share ideas, figure out priorities or identify the order in which tasks need to be approached;
✓ The group of four joins another group of four to share ideas;
✓ Each group feeds back to the whole class.

Jigsaw (Home/Expert) Groups

The 'Jigsaw' technique is a more complex way of structuring roles within a group. It is a very useful way of ensuring that all students contribute equally towards the success of a group task. Here's how it works:

✓ The topic for study is divided into different areas for research;
✓ You need the same number of areas of study as there are students in each group (i.e. if you have groups of 5, you need 5 areas for research);
✓ Each student is allocated a 'home' group – this is their main working group;

✓ Within the 'home' group each person is given a different area for their research – a subject on which they must become an 'expert';

✓ The 'experts' gather together and work as a team on researching their area;

✓ The 'experts' then report back to their home group on the expertise they have gathered;

✓ The 'home' groups work together on a joint task, with each expert inputting as appropriate on their area of expertise.

Different Group Roles

There are many different roles that you can ask your students to take on within their groups. The kind of roles you choose would depend on the type of activity you have set, and on the subject being taught. Some group activities will involve all the students working collaboratively, in very similar roles. However, for other group activities you may want to identify the roles that could or should be taken by each individual.

When we use groups in real life, beyond the school gates, it is often the case that there will be a group leader, who has some control over the input of the other members in the group. For instance, this is the role that a project leader takes on within a management consultancy project, or a chair within a committee. Depending on the nature of the skills and the subject you are trying to teach, it may be appropriate to elect group 'leaders', or to ask the students themselves to nominate the person that they wish to lead their group.

A useful way to designate and explain different roles is to use 'Role' cards. These describe the role that the student will play within the group, and give a 'job description' of what a person taking on that role needs to do. At the end of the activity the evaluation can include a focus on whether each person fulfilled the role that they had been set. The roles that you use might fall into one of the following categories:

✓ Ideas: generating, explaining, clarifying, linking, relating;
✓ Information: undertaking research, fact finding;
✓ Perspectives: opinions, beliefs, questioning viewpoints;
✓ Organisational: resources, timing and time keeping, group management, logistics;
✓ Evaluative: critic, feedback, setting standards;
✓ Motivational: energising, praising, focusing;
✓ Recorder: observer, note taker, scribe;
✓ Mediator: the group 'chair', listening to views, suggesting compromises, encouraging group to reach a consensus.

The Teacher's Role

In addition to helping the students learn to take on appropriate roles within each group, the teacher also has a vital role to play during collaborative learning. As the teacher you will need to take an overview of how the class is working as a whole. I find that it is a good idea, once the task has been set, to stand back for a minute or two and allow the students to settle to work.

Once the students have had this initial settling period, the following tips will help you take on a supportive role:

✓ Move around the groups ensuring they are on task. You can often do this by simply moving closer to a group as you pass – they will sense your presence.
✓ Avoid turning your back on the majority of the class at any one time. Position yourself where you can see most of the groups, and they can see you.

✓ Offer ideas or direction to the groups where needed but try not to intervene too early. Let your students have a chance to sort out problems for themselves before you offer your input. Be subtle with your interventions – your students will learn important lessons through making their own mistakes rather than always having you pre-empt them.

✓ Take care about 'hovering' beside a group to listen in to what is being said, as this can feel off-putting to students. I have found exactly the same happens when I am working with groups of teachers. The minute I come too close they 'seize up' or start saying what they think I want to hear.

✓ If you do feel you need to join a group, it works well to ask *'Is it okay if I sit with you/listen in/give some input?'* If there's a nervous laugh at this, or if the students don't seem ready for your input, then move on to the next group.

✓ If you feel that one group member is being destructive, or blocking the others from giving their ideas, encourage the other group members to deal with the situation. If you do have to talk with an individual, it may be best to do so privately, by taking the person away from the rest of the group to talk.

✓ Control the overall levels of noise within the room, and the noise levels of each group. The class as a whole will probably be unaware of the overall volume level because the students are busy talking with their own group. You can give an overview and help quieten things down as appropriate. As your students become more adept at group work, you can gradually encourage them to manage their own noise levels.

It can be a long hard job to ensure that your students show each other mutual respect and that everyone is making a contribution. Utilising group work is about building trust with and in your students. The only real way to build trust is to let your students have a go, even if sometimes this means that they mess things up or misbehave.

Role Play and Teacher 'In Role'

When we talk about 'role play' as a technique, what we mean is that the children take on a role that they would not normally play. This might be a character from a story; it could be a character found in real life, such as a detective or a scientist. Encourage your students to play around with the roles that they play when they are working within groups. They might:

✓ Take on a role that they would normally avoid, for instance taking on a high confidence role such as chairing or leading a group when they are actually quite shy.
✓ Take on a perspective that is not one they would usually hold, for instance speaking in a debate from a position that is the opposite to their true feelings.
✓ Understand or summarise why a character would feel or do certain things, or behave in a particular way, from within their role.

Sometimes you will want to take on a specific role *within* a group. This is often the case in an early years setting, where the teacher or practitioner role plays alongside the children. This technique is also useful in drama when doing a whole class improvisation in role, or when using a role of the expert scenario. The 'teacher in role' technique is useful because it allows you to:

✓ Guide and focus your students from within the group, as a character within the scenario;
✓ Offer input, advice or information without interrupting the flow of the action;
✓ Help the children build their thinking in a gentle and natural way.

There needs to be a degree of subtlety when using teacher in role, because otherwise your input can make the children freeze up, so that you limit rather than develop their learning. When you take on a role within a group, make sure that you:

✓ Listen in first to gain a sense of where the role play has got to already;
✓ Let the children guide you from within the drama, rather than imposing your ideas on them;
✓ Ask questions to move the learning on – 'could we try?' – rather than making statements – 'you should do this'.

Thinking Hats

Edward de Bono's 'Thinking Hats' technique is used in education, in business and in government. It is a method for encouraging people to consider a situation or question from all perspectives. As such, it can be useful for subjects that require the students to appreciate or take a variety of viewpoints on an issue. Often, when we discuss an issue in groups, we fall into the habit of taking our usual position. The 'thinking hats' offer a metaphorical framework to help us adopt different perspectives.

Each of the 'thinking hats' represents a type of viewpoint or way of thinking about an issue:

✓ White asks what information or facts are available;
✓ Red is the intuitive, instinctive or emotional response;
✓ Black is the logical approach, offering reasons for caution;
✓ Yellow is the optimistic approach, identifying reasons for optimism;
✓ Green is about creativity, provocations, and lateral thinking;
✓ Blue is about the management of the thinking processes.

The 'thinking hats' technique is useful for getting your students to discuss an issue in groups. They can do this 'wearing' each hat one after the other – looking first at the facts, then at their gut instincts, then at the reasons for caution, and so on. Or, with older students you might ask each member of the group to 'wear' one of the hats and speak from that perspective throughout the discussion.

With young children you might like to use actual hats to identify the roles (these are freely available online). Older students will very quickly understand that the hats are to be seen and used symbolically rather than literally.

The Third R:

Rights and Responsibilities

The Third R: Rights and Responsibilities

When you use group work, make it clear to your students that they have both rights and responsibilities. In turn, you as their teacher also have rights and responsibilities when you teach them via a group work format. The notion of a balance between the two aspects – that when learning, we have rights, but equally we have responsibilities – is a vital lesson for young people to understand.

Student Rights

Talk to and with your students about what their rights are, when they are working in groups. You might try talking this over during a whole class or small group discussion. Help your students identify what they can do if they feel that their group is not respecting their rights. Talk about the strategies that they should use *before* they turn to the teacher for help.

Students should have:

- ✓ The right for their voices to be heard in an equal and equitable way;
- ✓ The right to speak without interruption (within reason);
- ✓ The right for their ideas to be taken seriously, and for others to build on those ideas rather than denigrating them;
- ✓ The right for their ideas to be challenged, in a fair, polite and measured way;
- ✓ The right to challenge the ideas that others bring to the group, if they do not agree with them, again in a polite and sensitive way;
- ✓ The right to move laterally away from what might seem to be the main focus of the task, if they can justify why this lateral move should happen.

If they feel that their rights are not being respected the students might:

✓ Talk again about the roles that each group member is supposed to be taking on;
✓ Use a conch to ensure that all voices are heard;
✓ Ask the group to pause so that everyone can write down their ideas then take it in turns to read the ideas out;
✓ Explain how it feels when their ideas are not respected, or when no one listens to them.

Teacher Rights

A great rule of thumb for teachers is: 'Be reasonable, but don't reason with them.' As the adult in charge within the classroom, you have the right to expect certain behaviours, so long as the way that you run your classroom is reasonable. When you use group work, a key part of your role is to create an atmosphere where the students understand that they must work cooperatively. If you have done this, you have been reasonable, and therefore you do not need to negotiate your expectations of the attitudes and behaviour your students must demonstrate.

The teacher has:

✓ The right to format the groups as he or she decides is best, and for the students to work in these groupings without complaint;
✓ The right to experiment with different techniques and to take some risks when using group work, with the cooperation of the whole class;
✓ The right to expect that everyone will make their very best attempt to join in, to do their best, and to participate fully;

✓ The right to expect a reasonable level of noise, and to control the overall noise levels within the room so that others are not disturbed (both inside the classroom and beyond);

✓ The right to stop group work if students fail to take it seriously or refuse to focus on the task at hand;

✓ The right to set reasonable targets and expect that the students will do their best to meet them.

If your rights as a teacher are not being respected, you might:

✓ Pause the class to remind the students of their responsibilities;

✓ Clarify timings and targets to keep the students focused on the task;

✓ Explain that, if the students cannot work as required, you may need to stop the group activity;

✓ Re-establish the need for consideration for other students who are working in classes close by, particularly if noise levels are an issue;

✓ Stop the group work and set an individual task instead, explaining the attitudes you need to see before you can allow the students to return to the group activity again.

Student Responsibilities

It is vital for students to understand that the whole group is responsible for the success or failure of the task, not any one individual person. This will help them build the skill of collaboration, rather than trying to compete with each other to play the biggest part in the activity. The students need to understand that each person's input can and should benefit the group as a whole, and that they must work together to do well together.

In order to achieve this students have the responsibility to:

✓ Stay on task;

✓ Stick to the timings that have been given;

✓ Participate, with all members trying to input equally, and allowing others to give input in an equal way as well;

✓ Wait their turn to speak, and not talk over others, even if they feel frustrated when people need time to form or explain their ideas;

✓ Use a system or strategy as outlined (by the teacher or by the group) to ensure that all voices are heard;

✓ Look at and listen carefully to the person who is talking;

✓ Ask sensible questions to clarify what is being said;

✓ Build on other people's ideas with thoughts of their own;

✓ Take on board other people's ideas and arguments, and be willing to change their own views after listening to those of others, if they have been persuaded;

✓ Support others by listening willingly to their ideas and including them within the group;

✓ Reflect on and evaluate the learning done in groups, in order to improve it further in the future.

You will need to ensure that all students are accountable for their individual input into the activity. A useful way to do this is via a focused 'end product': for instance, a group presentation or an individual public performance. Find ways to evaluate how well each person contributed to the group effort as a whole. Peer assessment is a powerful tool for

achieving this (see the final section on 'Reflection' for more ideas).

A key responsibility for all concerned is to work together to achieve a shared goal. It is useful to remember that groups could be working towards different goals, shared only within their group, or that the groups within the whole class could be working together towards a common single goal.

For Example: In this 'haunted house' drama activity, the children must work cooperatively together in small groups, and then as a whole class group, in order for the final piece of drama to be successful. The objective of the activity is to help the students understand how to build a spooky atmosphere, full of dramatic tension. Divide the class up into groups: each group is going to form one room within the haunted house. Students act as haunted pieces of furniture or other items within their room – a chair, a painting, a grandfather clock, a bed, and so on. Each group decides on the furniture in their room, and how it is set out. The students then practise their spooky movements, and create accompanying sound effects.

The teacher then brings the class together and explains that two children have been dared to spend the night in a haunted house. Two volunteers are chosen to play the children and given a torch each so that they can find their way around. The activity needs to be done in semi-darkness, and it is particularly effective if you can create a total blackout in your room (e.g. in a drama studio that has blackout facilities). The other students take up their frozen positions as furniture in the different rooms of the house. They can add sound effects as and when they like, but they can only move as the children pass by them with their torches. As the children explore the house, they narrate their feelings and talk about what they see, building a whole class dramatised improvisation together. When done with the whole class working cooperatively, this exercise can be incredibly powerful and atmospheric.

Teacher Responsibilities

Of course it is not enough for the teacher to set a task and simply ask the groups to get on with it. Instead, the teacher must take responsibility for the success of the activity by creating a climate in which the task is clear, and everyone is required to contribute in order for a successful outcome to be achieved. The teacher needs to:

✓ Give a specific focus for group work, format the activity and groups appropriately, and explain the task clearly;

✓ Be specific about what he or she wants the students to achieve in their groups – be clear about the outcomes you expect to see;

✓ Explain to students the purpose behind them working together on a specific task, and the benefits that it will bring for them;

✓ Help the students learn how to build an atmosphere of teamwork, by being clear about what this means and giving them opportunities to achieve it;

✓ Have enough trust and faith in the students, in order to allow them to work independently;

✓ Build trust by accepting the risks inherent when doing group work, such as the possibility of off task behaviour or low-level disruption;

✓ Set ground rules and make it clear that all members of the group have a shared responsibility to follow these;

✓ Incorporate strategies and routines that will help all the students stay focused and on task.

The more quality group work that the children do, the better they will become at it. At first they may struggle to take turns, and to listen well to each other. This will depend on their age, the make-up of the class, the amount of group work they have done previously, and on their general attitudes to learning. However, if they are never given the chance to make mistakes, and to risk failure, there is no chance that they will ever improve their approach to collaborative learning.

A key part of the teacher's role is to figure out how much responsibility the students are able to take at any one time, and to find strategies to encourage them to become gradually more independent. Just as we might use Vygotsky's 'Zone of Proximal Development' to build each child's learning, so we can gradually increase the level of demand and difficulty that group activities place on our students.

The Fourth R:

Routines and Regulations

The Fourth R: Routines and Regulations

Over time, you can establish clear routines and regulations for group work: structures and rules that are repeated every time your students work in a group. These patterns will help your students learn to work more effectively and independently in groups. Gradually, as good habits become ingrained, you can decrease the amount of teacher input and guidance that the children need in order to be successful.

You can establish regulations and routines for all the organisational aspects of group work: creating groups, handling resources, arranging furniture, planning and managing time, controlling noise levels, taking turns and so on. Think ahead of time about how you will handle the organisational aspects of group work. This leaves you free to focus on supporting your students' learning.

Grouping Students

According to several studies, the optimum size of groups is around 4 to 6 students. If the group size is much larger than this, the students may lose focus while they wait to make an active contribution. If the group size is much smaller then there is less variety of student input, and the teacher may have a lot of different groups to visit during the course of the lesson.

When deciding how to group your students you need to consider:

✓ Whether to use teacher chosen groups, student chosen groups or a random method of selection (see the following section on 'Relationships' for more on this);

- ✓ Whether to mix ability levels within groups, to group the students according to ability, or to use some other method;
- ✓ If you do choose to group by ability, what specific 'ability' the group task requires to be done successfully;
- ✓ Whether there are any children who need additional support and how you will manage this;
- ✓ Whether it is best to group children needing extra support together, so that you can focus additional help on this one group;
- ✓ How you can achieve a mix of gender and cultural backgrounds within each group, as appropriate;
- ✓ How you will allocate adult support to individual children who have high levels of need;
- ✓ Whether you need to keep certain students apart because of the potential for behaviour issues or personality clashes.

How to Create Random Groups

If you choose to use random groupings, you need to have a method in place to create them. Here are some techniques for organising random groups:

- ✓ *Lolly sticks*: Ask each student to put his or her name on a lolly stick and place these in a pot that you keep on your desk. Draw sticks out of the pot to create different sizes and mixes of student groupings.
- ✓ *Playing cards*: Give each student a playing card as they enter the room. Depending on the size of the groups that you want, you could ask for those with the same suit to work together, or those with a specific number or picture card to work in the same group.

✓ *Coloured cards*: Have slips of coloured card and hand these out to the children as they enter, or alternatively place them on the desks before the class arrives. The students could work in a group with others who have the same coloured card, or alternatively they could be challenged to create a rainbow group.

You can use pretty much any kind of resource to indicate groupings: buttons, beads, shells, balls, toy animals – whatever takes your (and your children's) fancy.

Random Numbering System

This system helps you create groups of any size very quickly and easily, without the need for additional resources.

✓ Divide the number of students in the class by the number of groups you wish to create. For instance, if you have thirty students in the class and you want to create five groups, you would come up with the number six. (Note: don't worry if you have a number in your class that does not divide exactly, just pick the nearest whole number.)
✓ Ask the students to count around the room, up to this number. So, the first person would call out 'one', the next person 'two' and so on. When you reach 'six', the next person starts again at 'one'.
✓ Get all the students who called out the number 'one' to raise a hand. (This step is particularly important if you have a class of students who are likely to forget their number or pretend they had a different one.) Indicate the place in the classroom where group one will be working.

✓ Do the same for the rest of the numbers/groups. Finally ask all the students to go to the appropriate area of the classroom to join up with the other members of their group.

Keeping a Focus

You can help your students maintain their focus by being specific about the outcomes you want them to achieve. Use clear targets and set time constraints, to help your students focus on the task and to regulate their behaviour. Let your students know about:

✓ The overall academic goals or other objectives for the task;
✓ Any social or behavioural skills that you want them to focus on during the activity;
✓ The final deadline for the task, and interim deadlines for feedback as well;
✓ Any timings or time constraints that you are going to use;
✓ What the key targets are for the activity – including the criteria for really successful group work and outcomes;
✓ What will happen if individual students or groups drift off task – the consequences that will be used;
✓ How you will identify and/or reward those students who focus well on the task at hand, or who work particularly well in their groups.

Consider whether you should set the group task all at once, or whether you should split the longer activity up into smaller pieces, giving the students one part of the task at a time. Much will depend on how well your students can stay focused, and also on how much information they can retain at one time, and the nature of the activity that you want them to do.

Regulating Noise Levels

One of the biggest worries for some teachers about using group activities is the potential for lots of noise. When there are lots of children busy with their learning, it is almost inevitable that noise levels will rise. The key is to ensure that the noise is 'on task' talk, and that the teacher and students have strategies in place to manage the overall noise levels.

Consider who is going to regulate the noise levels. Although it is tempting for the teacher to do this, it is far better if you can get your students to regulate their own noise levels. Have several methods in place for pausing and re-gaining the students' attention as and when needed. For instance, you might use a non-verbal technique such as 'hands up' or a noise such as a bell.

There are a number of strategies that will help you achieve and maintain the right levels of noise:

✓ Before you set the students off on a group task, talk together about why it is important to maintain a reasonable level of noise. Identify the issues that excessive noise can cause – for instance, identifying any classes who are working close by. Talk about how a reasonable level of volume is vital for focused and effective learning.

✓ Once the students are on task in their groups, move freely around the room. Step in close to any groups who are struggling to stay focused or who cannot keep their volume levels down. Stay quiet at first, as it may be that your presence will remind them to regulate their noise. If not, intervene and set a clear target for the right level of volume.

✓ Use a stop and respond approach, where you draw the class together for regular feedback during group activities. This helps maintain focus and also avoids the rise in levels of noise that occurs naturally over time.

✓ When you pull the students together, use this time to gain and give feedback about their work thus far, to discuss any issues they have with understanding what they are meant to do, or to check that everyone is taking on an appropriate role within the group. You can also remind the students about timing to keep them focused and on track.

✓ Consider creating a 'noise-o-meter': this is a visual indicator of rising levels of noise. You could simply use a graph on the board that shows how the noise is rising and have a 'line above which noise levels must not cross'. If you prefer a more high tech solution, you can buy electronic sets of traffic lights that change colour as the decibel levels rise, with an alarm that goes off at a preset limit.

✓ You might also allocate one student within each group to take on the role of 'noise monitor'. This person could take responsibility for ensuring that the group's volume level does not get too high.

Boosting Student Self-Regulation

Individual accountability is one of the key factors in effective group work. When students know that their individual contributions will be checked by their teacher or by their peers, they are more likely to make an equitable contribution to the activity. Before you start work on a group task, ask your students to identify the kind of helpful and unhelpful behaviours that they might display. Encourage them to set themselves targets, based around those behaviours that they find hardest to maintain. At the end of the task, ask the students to assess which of these behaviours they showed, and whether there were any that they did not manage to achieve.

You can find more on boosting student regulation, and evaluating individual and group outcomes, in the final section of this book on 'Reflection'.

Dealing with Resources

Give responsibility for handling resources to your students: ask that they collect what they need at the start of the lesson and tidy it away again at the end. This boosts their independent learning skills, and it saves you time and energy. When you are evaluating the learning that your students do in groups, include a reference to how well the groups managed and handled resources.

In order to do deal with resources you might:

✓ Ask each group to allocate one person who is responsible for picking up and tidying away the resources – the 'organiser' or 'resource monitor'.
✓ Have a 'job role' card that indicates the key responsibilities of the resource monitor, and hand these out randomly, one to a member of each group.
✓ Offer the chance to hand out resources as a useful motivator for those who are working or behaving well. (This is usually a popular volunteer task, particularly in the early years setting and at primary school.)
✓ Where you need to use a large number of resources for an activity, ask that everyone works together as a class team to hand them out and tidy them away.

✓ Have a clearly structured time frame for clearing away resources. You could use music such as the 'Mission Impossible' theme tune to give a focus to tidy up time.

Ensure that you have sufficient resources for everyone to access: this is particularly important if your students are going to be using texts for research, or they need to use ICT equipment to complete the task. Remember, too, that people are a very valuable resource within the classroom. Consider carefully how you can make best use of any support staff who are working with you. Ask these staff to give input into deciding on the kind of roles that they would like to take on during group activities.

Setting Tasks

Often you will want to set up a group task by explaining it to the whole class simultaneously: for many activities this is the simplest and quickest way. If your students are new to group work it is probably best for you to spend time talking with them as a whole class about what the task is and how they should approach it. You can also experiment with other ways of setting activities, to build student independence and to increase pace and motivation.

As an alternative to whole class explanations, you could:

✓ Put all the instructions into an envelope and let the students get straight onto task as soon as they get in their groups.
✓ Have the instructions showing on your whiteboard when the students enter the room. You might include a target for how quickly they can read the instructions and settle down to their learning.

✓ Start with a concise key question or activity suggestion, but encourage the students to think laterally and devise their own ways of approaching the question or task.

✓ Have a list of tasks that you give to each group, but leave the groups to decide on the best method and order for completing those tasks.

Taking Turns

Learning how to take turns is often one of the hardest aspects of group work for students. When children are young, the urge to be the one to be in charge, or for their own voice to be heard, is very powerful indeed. Some children do not learn to control this impulse as they grow older: they cannot defer gratification, they want an instant reward. You might have noticed how some students always call out or demand to go first.

Interestingly, it is quite often the most academically able students who find it hardest to take turns when working in groups. The brightest students want to let everyone else know what the answer is, or tell everyone else what to do. For these children, group work is as much about learning vital social skills as it is about a focus on academic development.

There are various ways to help children develop the ability to take turns. For instance you could:

✓ Have a 'conch' for each group (an indicator of who has the 'right' to speak at any one time). Your conch can be any interesting object – a shell, a talking stick, a toy, a 'turn to talk' card, etc.

✓ Give each group a timer and set a time limit for how long each person can speak at any one time.

✓ Have a marker of some kind (coins, cards, etc.) that each child must cash in when they wish to speak. Once they have used all their markers they must let everyone else have their turn to talk before starting over again.

✓ Mark the passage of time for the class yourself, for instance by ringing a bell at intervals to indicate when it is time for the next person to speak.

✓ Number the students within their groups. When you call out a particular number, only the students with that number can talk.

Routines for Whole Class Group Work

Teaching techniques such as 'circle time', 'carpet time' and whole class discussions are a form of group work, albeit one that takes place with the whole class working together. When you use these formats, it is important to allow as many voices to be heard as possible. Routines and structures will help you ensure that the children use this format in the very best possible way.

Routines for Circle Time

Circle time is a very popular technique in early years settings and primary classrooms, and also in drama lessons. To get the most out of circle time sessions:

✓ Ask the children to make a very clear and round circle shape – thus allowing everyone to be seen and heard. This creates a sense of high expectations for behaviour and attitudes to learning, and makes the statement that 'we do things properly here'.

✓ Sometimes, break with convention and keep your children on their toes by going anti-clockwise around the circle.

✓ When you ask everyone to make a contribution in turn around the circle, give the children the option to 'pass'. This avoids the shy children, and those with limited language skills, feeling as though they have been put on the spot.

Routines for Using the Space

The way that you manage the space will have a direct impact on the quality of the group work that can take place. If your classroom is set up with desks in rows, and you want your students to work in groups larger than pairs, then you will need to rearrange the furniture. This is not an insurmountable problem. Anyone who has taught drama in a classroom can attest to the fact that students are happy to move the desks and chairs if they are sufficiently motivated. Indeed, working as a team to rearrange the furniture is a useful example of why equity of labour is vital for successful group work.

Sometimes you may need to group your desks together; other times you could put them into a U shape so that the whole class can debate as one group. You might also want the room entirely cleared of furniture to leave a space in the middle. If you have to teach in other people's classrooms, or if you share a room with one or more other teachers, then leave sufficient time to return the space to its previous layout. Before you move another teacher's furniture, draw a quick sketch of how the room looks – it is surprisingly easy to forget what it looked like after a busy lesson.

Here are two other ways to 'use the space' for effective group work:

✓ Set up a 'Gallery Walk', where questions are posed around the room. Ask the groups of students to visit the questions and to leave their answers on them. As the students move around the room, they read other people's answers before adding their own.

✓ Use the 'doughnut' technique for gathering and sharing ideas. With this technique each group nominates a scribe to write down their ideas. The scribe has a few minutes with the starter group before moving on to the next table. After the scribe has visited all the tables, he or she reports back with the ideas to the original group.

The Fifth R:

Relationships

The Fifth R: Relationships

Group work is great for boosting relationships within a class: both the relationship between the teacher and the students, and also the relationships between the students themselves. Through using group work, the teacher can build an ethos of cooperation and consideration. This ethos will take a while to create, because it is about building genuine, long-term relationships. Do not despair or give up if it does not happen as quickly as you would like.

A very useful ethos for group work is: 'In this class we work with everybody and anybody.' Ideally you want the students to feel like they are working together as a team, rather than competing to outdo each other. If your children complain when they are put into a particular group, repeat your mantra: 'In this class we work with everybody and anybody' and then carry on as before.

By using group work you help your students build an understanding of the social context within which we live. They learn how positive, respectful relationships are the glue that bonds our society together. They learn how to work with others, regardless of who they are or what they are like. They see that we must both give and receive help, that we can negotiate our role within a social context, and that we should consider how our behaviour makes other people feel. All these are key skills in developing positive relationships and all will feed into a collaborative classroom atmosphere.

Types of Relationship

There are obvious differences between the teacher/student relationship, and that between students and their peers. The peer relationship is generally much more informal, and more evenly balanced in terms of status. When two children talk

46

together, they can understand what the other is saying in a straightforward and direct way. They speak the equivalent of a common language.

When you get your students to learn in a group, the sense of peer responsibility they feel can be a very powerful motivator. Where the success of the whole task rests on each individual's input, then many students will feel that they owe it to their peers to work as hard as possible. If peer relationships are strong within the class, the idea that students do not want to let their peers down can be a powerful influence on their behaviour and learning.

Positive Group Relationships

Our aim as teachers is to create an atmosphere of respect, collaboration and support. We want to foster the kind of relationships that benefit the learning and well-being of all members of the group. The 'Rights and Responsibilities' outlined in the third part of this book are crucial for doing this. Talk with your children about what a 'positive group relationship' looks like. Introduce key attitudes/attributes and ask your students to assess how well they have achieved these aspects during their group work.

You might talk about how you want your students to be:

✓ Supportive
✓ Collaborative
✓ Considerate
✓ Inclusive
✓ Fair

Negative Group Relationships

Keep an eye out for any students who bring the following negative attitudes or approaches to group work. Intervene with individuals and use whole class discussions to identify why these roles are potentially damaging. Use peer group feedback and evaluation after an activity is completed, to encourage students to reward those who take on positive roles within the group.

Negative approaches would include students who are:

* ✗ Keen to take over – students who dominate the group, telling the other group members what to do;
* ✗ Aggressive – being rude or abusive towards other group members;
* ✗ Blocking – stopping the group from moving onwards with the task;
* ✗ Attention seeking – drawing attention to themselves rather than allowing everyone to have equal input;
* ✗ Distracting – trying to pull the group away from focusing on the task, perhaps through misbehaviour;
* ✗ Opting out – allowing the other members of the group to do all the work, without making any contributions.

Some students hate group work because they feel they are 'above' it and because they want to work alone to achieve the maximum grades. They do not want other students (who they perhaps perceive as 'slower') to hold them back or bring them down. An interesting method for dealing with these students is to *put them in a group together*. Because all the students have a similar attitude to group work, they are forced to learn to cooperate and negotiate, so that they do not fail at the task.

How to Counter Blocking

All the negative approaches described above can limit the quality of group work that takes place. Here is a great activity that will help you counter the student who continually blocks the forward progress of the group. This drama/speaking and listening activity shows students how they can take responsibility for moving their group onwards.

This is how it works:

✓ Divide the students up into pairs: one person is 'A' and the other 'B';
✓ Student A is going to try and persuade student B to do something;
✓ For instance, A wants to persuade B to go into town with her that evening.

The first time that you run this exercise, student B must respond to every suggestion with 'No'. Whatever A suggests, B must give a firm negative in response. For instance:

A: *We could go to the cinema tonight, couldn't we?*
B: *No.*
A: *Well, we could go out for a meal together, couldn't we?*
B: *No.*
A: *How about if we go and play in the park for a bit?*
B: *No.*

Once the students have done this for a few minutes, pull the class back together and ask how it felt to have the response 'no' to every suggestion they made. Now run the activity a second time. Student A carries on making suggestions, but this time student B is going to say 'yes but' in response, giving a reason why the suggestion isn't a good idea.

So the activity might run something like this:

A: *We could go to the cinema tonight, couldn't we?*

B: *Yes, but there's nothing good on so there's no point.*
A: *Well, we could go out for a meal together, couldn't we?*
B: *Yes, but I've got a sore tooth so it's really painful for me to eat.*
A: *How about if we go and play in the park for a bit?*
B: *Yes, but they said on the weather forecast that it's going to rain later.*

Again, talk about how it felt to have every suggestion greeted with a negative response. Now run the activity a final time. Student B is going to say 'yes and' to every suggestion, adding their own ideas to those of their friend. So, the final version might sound something like this:

A: *We could go to the cinema tonight, couldn't we?*
B: *Yes, and afterwards we could go for some food.*
A: *How about if we go and play in the park for a bit first?*
B: *Yes, and then we can see if there's anyone there who wants to come with us to the cinema.*

Again, discuss how this felt with your students. They should notice that, by accepting and then building on each other's ideas, everyone feels more positive and they are likely to develop far more interesting ideas together.

Getting into Groups

For each group task you need to make a decision about whether you should use random groupings, allocate groupings yourself, or allow the students to choose the groups in which they work. The choice you make will depend on lots of different factors, including:

✓ The relationships your students already have with each other;
✓ The ethos that you want to build;

50

✓ The age group you are teaching;

✓ The subject area or topic that you are studying;

✓ How well motivated your students are;

✓ The kind of mix of abilities you have in your class;

✓ How far social interactions filter into or disrupt learning in your lessons.

There are advantages and disadvantages to getting into groups in different ways, both in terms of building relationships, and also in terms of the learning that will take place. For instance, in drama lessons I have found it works well to insist on completely random groupings right from the very start. If you never offer any other approach as an alternative, it does not even occur to the students that it might be possible to pick groups in any other way.

You might like to try asking your students what they think the best way to get into groups would be, for a particular task. Consider too whether there would be benefits in keeping your groups the same over time, for instance when working on long term group projects.

Here are some thoughts about the positives and negatives of different approaches to choosing groups, and the kind of activities for which they might be most useful.

Random Groupings

Advantages: This can throw up some very interesting and challenging mixes of students; it creates an ethos of 'everybody works with anybody'; over time, all students should end up working together with everyone else in the class.

Disadvantages: Sometimes clashes may occur between individuals, and you need to be confident that you can handle these.

Works well for: Creative subjects and groups of students who need to learn to work in a more collaborative way.

Teacher Allocated Groupings

Advantages: This helps to limit the amount of differentiation needed in subjects such as literacy; the teacher can aim for the right mix of abilities and personalities; set groupings give a sense of continuity over time.

Disadvantages: This relies heavily on the teacher's knowledge of the individual students – both their personalities and their ability levels; it can also lead to a static situation where groups rarely mix.

Works well for: Literacy and numeracy in a primary class with a wide mix of abilities; group activities where there are a number of clearly defined roles that would be suited to particular students.

Student Chosen Groupings

Advantages: Students tend to feel more relaxed when they are working with their friends; where cohesion and collaboration are already at least partly in place, being allowed to choose groups can be used as a reward or a motivator for hard working students.

Disadvantages: Less popular students may get left out of groupings; this approach can limit the development of collaborative working, as students do not try to work with those outside their normal social group.

Works well for: Older students and highly motivated classes, where there are no students likely to be left out; GCSE tasks in creative subject areas where achieving good collaboration is the key to success.

The Sixth R:

Rich

The Sixth R: Rich

Group work can be 'rich' in every sense of the word. It can offer enrichment through the broadness and depth of the learning that takes place. It gives a chance for students to experiment with and learn a richer and wider palette of language structures and vocabulary. It can also be an opportunity for the teacher to incorporate a really great range of high quality resources as an inspiration for learning.

Rich Talk

Ideally, we want the talk that takes place within groups to be as rich as possible: in the vocabulary that the children use, in the way that they structure thinking, and also in the methods that they use to develop their ideas. The students should be clear that group work is not about competitive arguments but is about sharing information and thinking, in order to solve problems or develop ideas together.

The students at the lower end of the ability range, and those who lack confidence, will often struggle to use language well when asked to talk about their thinking. Group work is great for allowing them to rehearse their ideas with their peers. This approach feels less pressurised to them than being asked to speak out in front of the whole class.

Help your students understand that we can use talk for different purposes, and that as our purposes vary, so does the kind of talk that we should use. Within a group discussion, we might be using language to describe, to persuade, to explain, to recount, to agree or disagree, to reason, to make inferences, and so on. The kind of vocabulary and language structures we use will vary according to the purpose of our talk. Encourage your students to reflect on the kind of language that they use when they are working in groups.

To encourage rich talk, try the following strategies:

- ✓ Record one or more of the group discussions and ask the students to listen back to it after the activity is completed. Ask them to evaluate the kind of vocabulary they used and how well they explained their ideas.
- ✓ Give the students a list of key words or vital vocabulary that you would like them to use, in the appropriate context, during a group work activity. You could offer them a tick list, or some word cards that they can play when they use the words.
- ✓ Encourage your students to use Standard English when discussing their ideas in groups. When they take on an 'expert role' this will usually encourage them to do this (see the first section on 'Roles' for more on the 'role of the expert').
- ✓ Teach your students the 'SEE' technique. For each **statement** they make, they must give **evidence** to support it and **explain** how their evidence backs up the statement they have made.
- ✓ Help your students develop their use of questioning techniques. Remember that this is not necessarily a skill that will come easily to them. The 'Socractic' techniques described below are very useful for improving their questioning skills.

Socratic Questioning Techniques

One of the keys to rich talk is to get the students asking the right kind of questions of each other, within their groups. Questions make thinking visible – they allow your students to get below the surface of a subject, issue or opinion and explore it in all its complexity. Socrates is renowned as one of the founders of Western philosophy. His idea was that we should solve problems by asking ourselves questions, in order to explore our beliefs, and in doing so to find answers.

Socratic questioning techniques are ones that encourage the teacher, and his or her students, to dig down beneath a question, or a dilemma, or a problem, and ask questions until a solution is discovered or a conclusion/consensus is reached. These techniques are useful in helping your students develop rich talk within their group work.

When using Socratic questioning, you and your students should:

✓ Respond to all answers with a further question;
✓ Treat all thoughts as in need of development;
✓ Assume that all questions are based on answers to prior questions;
✓ Pursue connections between thoughts – see all thinking as linked.

These Socractic techniques will encourage you and your students to examine the assumptions, agendas, inferences, concepts, points of view and information behind the way that they think. The teacher can model this approach for the students during whole class question and answer sessions or when working alongside individual children. For instance, you might:

✓ Ask questions to encourage your students to clarify a key concept or idea;
✓ Challenge any assumptions and misconceptions your students make when they explain their thinking;
✓ Encourage them to develop their arguments by supporting any statements with evidence;

✓ Look at alternative perspectives, for instance by approaching a question from a range of viewpoints.

Sustained Shared Thinking

The technique of sustained shared thinking is a particularly rich kind of group work discussion activity. This technique is widely used in the early years sector, where the adult works alongside the child, helping the child to build ideas by asking appropriate questions and offering a scaffold within which ideas can be expressed. Because there are high adult to child ratios in early years settings, practitioners are freed up to spend time working closely with individuals, or groups of children, to scaffold and develop their thinking.

Sustained shared thinking is about working together with a child to:

✓ Solve problems (sometimes the practitioner will create a fictional problem for the child to solve – this is referred to as a provocation);
✓ Clarify concepts – the practitioner inputs the appropriate information or knowledge at just the right moment, or helps the child address any misconceptions;
✓ Build narratives – the adult works with the children to create a story together, in which they are usually immersed as characters;
✓ Evaluate activities – the practitioner helps the child evaluate what they have done or learned thus far, and build on it further;
✓ Ask appropriate questions – the adult poses a question that will help the child move the thinking onwards, or take the conceptual understanding to a deeper level.

Rich Tasks and Activities

When we decide to use group work for an activity in class, it is important that we use this format because it is the most appropriate one for the task that is to be done. When you decide to do an activity in a group, ask yourself: does doing this in a group format actually add to the learning? Does it help me achieve a specific learning objective, and does it best suit this particular kind of activity?

The richest tasks are those that:

✓ Are complex enough for all students to have to work together to achieve a good end result;
✓ Incorporate shared goals that can only be achieved if the students collaborate;
✓ Include a requirement to solve problems, or develop higher order thinking, or have some other clear learning outcome that is best achieved in a group format;
✓ Create or enhance a feeling of curiosity, motivation and deep interest in a topic or subject area;
✓ Give an opportunity for the groups to feedback to the whole class, whether through talk or through an end product of some description;
✓ Encourage the students to evaluate what they have achieved, and how they could achieve even more the next time around.

Rich Memory

Group work is very useful indeed for helping your students retain new information. When we anchor new knowledge to existing knowledge, we can retain it more easily in the longer term. Similarly, when we learn something new in a context in which it will be used, it is easier for us to remember it.

The sooner we can practise what we have learned, and get feedback on it, the better we will remember it.

To boost memory, get your students to:

✓ Use examples, analogies and anecdotes within their groups, talking about how new information links to something that they already know;
✓ Organise information in ways that will help them retain it – by creating mnemonics, or summarising it and explaining it to the rest of the group or class;
✓ Work within real life contexts, relating what they learn to their home lives, their families, and sharing their ideas about how this might happen within their groups;
✓ Apply new learning and gain feedback on it immediately, from their peers within their groups, as well as from their teacher.

It is worth remembering that, by using the 'processing power' of all the students in your class simultaneously, you boost the learning of the maximum number of people. If all the students are relying on your thinking as their teacher, then this may limit how much individuals can achieve.

Rich Resources

Resources can add hugely to the students' engagement with and interest in group work, as well as focusing their minds on the task at hand. When you get your students to use resources, there are various management issues that you need to address. See the fourth part of this guide, on 'Routines and Regulations' for more on 'Dealing with Resources'. Often, the 'richest' resources are not those that cost a lot of money, but those that require creative and lateral thinking either to find or to use.

The richest resources might:

✓ Surprise or delight or fascinate the children;
✓ Be simple so that they push the students to think laterally, for instance cardboard boxes (for dens, etc.) or empty plastic bottles (to build a greenhouse, etc.);
✓ Appeal to all the senses, being colourful, or highly textured, or harnessing the students' sense of smell;
✓ Help give structure to the activity, for example through the use of sand timers;
✓ Incorporate an element of fun, for instance a quiz or a board game;
✓ Offer complexity to the very able, by presenting them with a challenge, for instance a difficult piece of text given to those groups with the strongest readers;
✓ Offer support for the less able, by giving them a scaffold within which to build their ideas, for instance a writing frame that the group must complete or a set of key word cards to use.

The Seventh R:

Reflection

The Seventh R: Reflection

When we reflect on the work that we have done, and we evaluate how well it went, we learn important lessons about how to get better at it. Use plenty of feedback, reflection and evaluation both during and after group work. This will help your students get better at working in groups, and also encourage them to improve the learning they achieve in groups over time.

Two key questions that you want students to consider are: what kind of individual contribution did they make to their group and the learning, and how well did the group itself work together as a unit? The following questions will help you guide your students to reflect on and evaluate what went on during a group activity:

- ✓ What did we as a group do well here?
- ✓ What did we do that was not so successful, and why?
- ✓ What did I as an individual do well here?
- ✓ What did I do that was not so successful, and why?
- ✓ Did we all make an equitable contribution to the group activity?
- ✓ If we did not, what stopped us from achieving this?
- ✓ How can we develop our learning further in the future, and improve the outcomes we achieve?
- ✓ Did we fulfil the roles that we were meant to take on within the group?
- ✓ What is the quality of our end product like?

Evaluating Contributions

You need to find a way of regulating and evaluating the individual contributions that students make to group activities. This can be tricky for the teacher, because you cannot hope to keep an eye on all the students at any one time. You can use markers or tokens to help scaffold and regulate the learning that your students do in their groups, and to evaluate the contribution that each person made.

To do this:

✓ Give a set of tokens to each student. These could be any form of counters – buttons, coins, cards, etc. It works well if each individual student within a group has a different kind of counter.

✓ Each time a group member makes a contribution during the group task, they place one of their counters in the centre of the table.

✓ At the end of the activity, if all group members have made an equal contribution, there will be an equal set of markers in the middle.

A great idea for motivating older students is to use Euros or other coins as markers. You can also motivate your students by giving extra tokens as rewards. For instance, if you spot an example of good listening, or a student who is speaking really confidently, you might award that person an additional counter. You can also 'fine' groups or individuals if they are not on task, by taking away some of their counters.

When setting a group task that involves written input from the whole group, a great strategy for checking on individual contributions is to give different coloured marker pens to different students. At the end of the activity a quick glance at the group's written work will show you exactly which students have contributed most to this aspect of the task.

Evaluating Roles

When you have asked your students to take on a specific role within the group, it is important to evaluate what happened afterwards. Talk about and evaluate the roles that the students took on. Were they successful in their role? Did they find a particular kind of role hard? Was their role a challenge for them or not? What kind of role might they want or need to try out next time around to develop further?

At the end of a task, you can also ask the members of each group to decide who deserves a reward for their work in their role. For instance, you might give the group ten counters to distribute amongst their team, according to how well each individual fulfilled the role that they had been given. Students are usually surprisingly honest, fair and often very tough in their assessment of their group's work.

Evaluating Outcomes

You will also need to find methods to get your students to evaluate the learning that took place, and for you to assess that learning as well. A useful way to do this is to ask the students to produce an end product as part of the group activity. By asking the students to produce a product that will be evaluated, you can also boost motivation and improve levels of effort. This end product could take a variety of different forms. For instance, it could be:

✓ A Powerpoint or other kind of presentation summarising what they have learned;
✓ A scrapbook style document including writing, photographs, samples of materials, and so on;
✓ A proposal style document created from within an expert role, that they must present to a 'client';

✓ A sculpture for display within a school arts or sculpture trail;

✓ A presentation or performance to be given during a school assembly;

✓ A lesson activity that they are going to teach to the rest of the class;

✓ A written document – this could be a magazine, a book, a pamphlet, etc.

Where written documents are published in some way to a real life audience, for instance of parents or of other students, this will maximise the motivation to achieve a great end result.

By using the strategies explained in this mini guide, and by having a measure of trust and faith in your students, you should be able to make your group work truly 'great'.